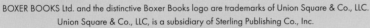

BOXER BOOKS Ltd. and the distinctive Boxer Books logo are trademarks of Union Square & Co., LLC.
Union Square & Co., LLC, is a subsidiary of Sterling Publishing Co., Inc.

Illustrations © 2012 Britta Teckentrup
Text © 2012 Boxer Books Limited

This edition first published in North America in 2023 by Boxer Books Limited.
Originally published as *Big Noisy Book of Busy Places* in 2012.

ISBN 978-1-912757-92-3

Library of Congress Control Number: 2022952438

For information about custom editions, special sales, and premium purchases,
please contact specialsales@unionsquareandco.com.

Printed in China
Lot #:
2 4 6 8 10 9 7 5 3 1
06/23

unionsquareandco.com
Text written by Harriet Blackford.
The illustrations were prepared using hand-painted paper and digital collage.

BIG BOOK OF CITIES

Illustrated by
Britta Teckentrup

Written by
Harriet Blackford

Boxer Books

CITIES

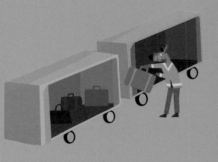

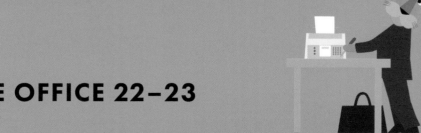

THE SCHOOL
Welcome to the city school.

Excited children hang up their coats and bags.

Playground assistants watch over the children while the teachers take a break.

In art class the teacher shows students how to mix paints.

The caretaker takes care of the school building. One of the children has left a soccer ball on a roof.

After school, there's practice for the school play.

"Good morning," says the teacher. "Good morning," says the class. Today they are learning geography.

The librarian helps children choose good books.

In science class, the children turn on a light bulb with a battery.

When the bell rings, children line up in the cafeteria. The cooks have been busy making lunch in the kitchen.

THE SHOPPING CENTER

It's busy, busy in this huge shopping mall!

The escalators take shoppers up and down. ♪♫

At the shoe store, the salesperson makes sure new shoes fit just right.

In the music store, a musician tunes up a new guitar.

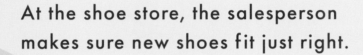

The furniture store manager takes a new delivery.

At night, maintenance crews clean the center for tomorrow's shoppers.

If the bookstore doesn't have a book in stock, the bookseller can order it for you.

The toy store salesperson steers a remote control car all around the store.

The security guards lock the doors.

Delivery trucks bring new goods to the loading dock. Workers fill their carts with boxes and deliver them to all the stores.

THE GARAGE
All cities have garages.

A fuel tanker truck delivers fuel.

The driver attaches the hose to an underground tank that feeds gasoline to all the pumps.

A busy worker at the car wash polishes the cars and vacuums the rugs.

Some cars need gasoline or diesel.

Many new cars only use electricity. Much better for the environment.

The car carrier delivers brand-new cars to the showroom. Many of these cars are electric, which is much healthier for us.

A delivery person fills up the vending machine with cold drinks.

Oh dear! The car won't start. But the smart mechanic knows what to do.

The mechanic raises the car on the hydraulic lift to look underneath.

THE SWIMMING POOL
Pools are fun places to exercise.

The lifeguard can see everything from her high chair. She is there in case anyone needs help.

An attendant sells tickets.

"Keep kicking!" shouts the swimming instructor from the side of the pool.

Be careful! The cleaner has just washed the floor in the changing room.

The showers are too cold! A maintenance person fixes them.

At the toddler pool, an instructor helps children put on water wings.

The pool technician collects a water sample to make sure the pool is clean.

A big inflatable octopus needs more air. Pool staff use a pump to inflate it.

THE THEATER

This is a great place to see plays and shows, and to hear singers.

Plays are stories acted by actors on a stage.

High on a platform above the stage, the lighting crew adjusts the lights.

A sound technician adjusts the microphone.

Stagehands move the scenery into place.

Musicians in the orchestra pit tune their instruments.

It's busy in the dressing rooms!
Actors change into their costumes.

The makeup artist
paints actors' faces.
Everyone is ready.

The wardrobe
manager has done
a great job.

Outside the theater,
a maintenance person
checks the
title of
the play.

People line up
to buy tickets at
the box office.

The usher
checks tickets
and shows
everyone to
their seats.

Vendors
sell snacks
before the
play starts.

17

THE AIRPORT

Today, we are looking at ways to make air travel better for the planet.

On the runways, emergency vehicles are always ready.

The pilot checks the airplane controls. The navigator checks the route maps.

The flight attendant demonstrates safety procedures.

Time to board!

Passengers weigh their luggage at the check-in counter.

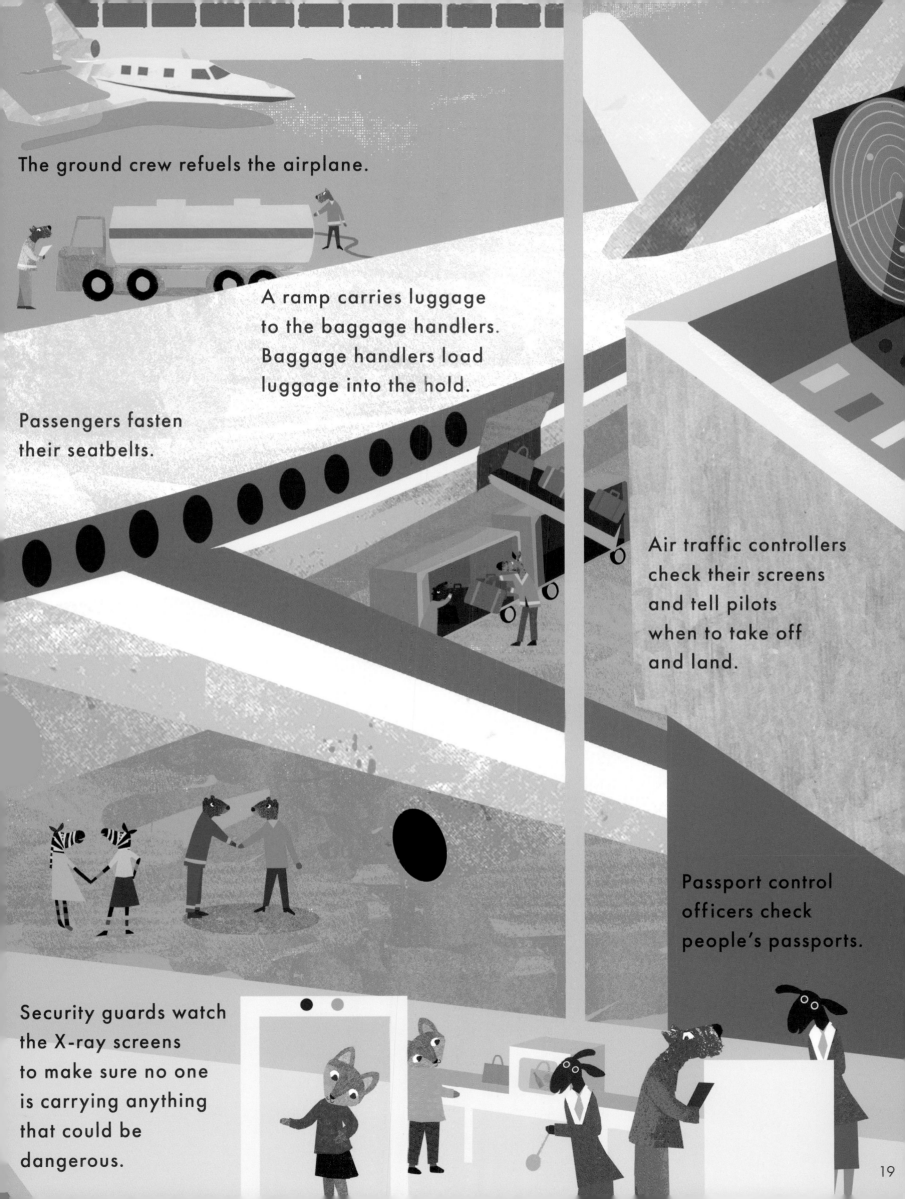

The ground crew refuels the airplane.

A ramp carries luggage to the baggage handlers. Baggage handlers load luggage into the hold.

Passengers fasten their seatbelts.

Air traffic controllers check their screens and tell pilots when to take off and land.

Passport control officers check people's passports.

Security guards watch the X-ray screens to make sure no one is carrying anything that could be dangerous.

THE HOSPITAL
This is the best place to be if you are unwell or injured.

The doctor goes on rounds each day to see how the patients are feeling.

"You are so brave," says the nurse, taking a blood sample.

The ambulance driver stops in front of the emergency department at the hospital.

The paramedics jump out and wheel the patient in.

Scientists in the laboratories check samples with their microscopes.

Technicians use X-ray machines, scanners, and ultrasound to see inside patients.

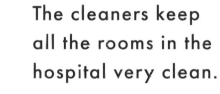

In the operating room, the surgeon scrubs up and the nurse lays out the instruments.

The cleaners keep all the rooms in the hospital very clean.

"Good-bye," says the doctor, handing a new baby to parents.

THE OFFICE

People do all kinds of work in offices.

The inventor tries out a new kettle.

The photocopier seems very noisy.

Oh no! The printer isn't working. Call maintenance!

Pick up some fruit and a sandwich for lunch!

Need any milk?

In the boardroom, the bosses meet to discuss important plans.

"Good morning," says the receptionist.

Many office workers have a desk to work at and can use their laptops.

Be fit and take the stairs, or be quick and take the elevator.

THE FACTORY

Factories make things we want. This factory makes cakes.

This baker checks the recipe.

The controller programs the machines.

Churn the batter.

Squirt it out.

Bake in the giant ovens.

This factory makes cars.

48

The designers and engineers check the car plans.

The operator sets up huge robotic machines.

Here goes . . . Press out shapes.

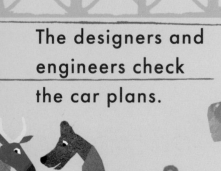

24

Squeeze on the filling.

Roll by hand.

Here comes the icing.

Through the slicing machine.

Decorations are added to the cake.

The cakes are packed in boxes, ready to eat!

Weld parts together.

Test drive the car. It's ready to go!

Spray on the paint.

Fasten in the seats.

THE BUILDING SITE

This building site is very busy and noisy.

Careful on the scaffolding!

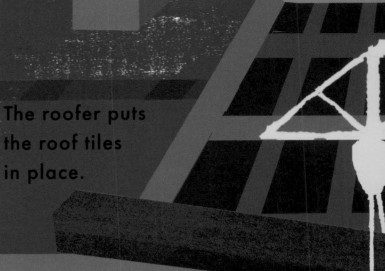

The roofer puts the roof tiles in place.

The electrician lays the cables that make the lights and sockets work.

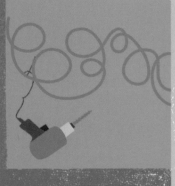

The carpenter cuts a piece of wood for the staircase.

The plumber installs the pipes to carry the water. Hooray—no leaks!

The plasterer spreads plaster on the walls to make them smooth.

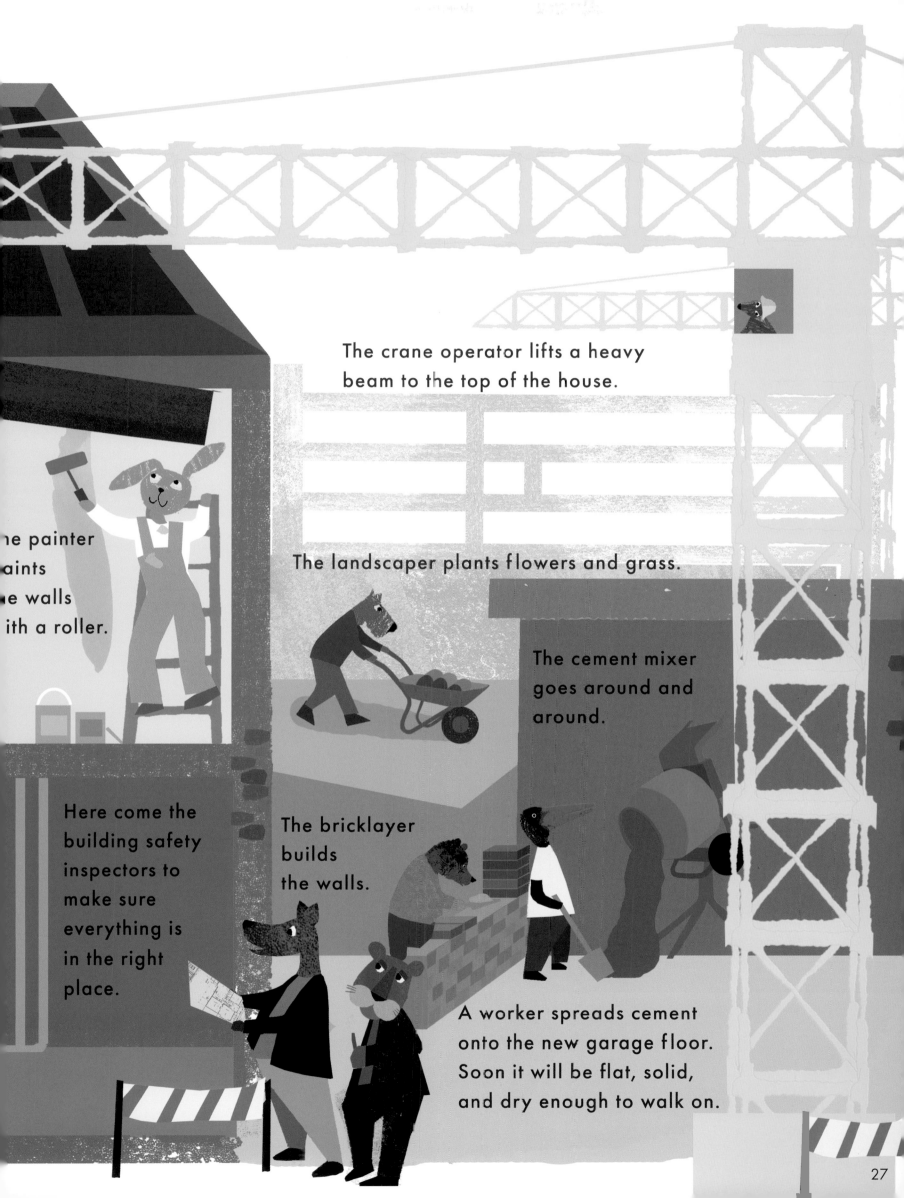

The crane operator lifts a heavy beam to the top of the house.

The painter paints the walls with a roller.

The landscaper plants flowers and grass.

The cement mixer goes around and around.

Here come the building safety inspectors to make sure everything is in the right place.

The bricklayer builds the walls.

A worker spreads cement onto the new garage floor. Soon it will be flat, solid, and dry enough to walk on.

THE POLICE STATION

Police officer help to keep us safe and arrest thieves

They rush through traffic in their police cars, sounding the sirens, to get to an accident.

Traffic officers close roads where a crime has been committed or where an accident has occurred.

Forensic scientists look at every little detail of a crime scene for clues.

At the laboratory, technicians examine the clues.

Police helicopter pilots use bright lights to catch a burglar at night.

Police dogs are trained to work with the police and catch criminals.

Dogs have a fantastic sense of smell and are able to sniff out trouble.

In a courtroom, a jury is made up of 12 people.

All rise for the judge!

The jury listens to all the evidence and decides whether a suspect is guilty or not guilty.

THE POST OFFICE

Most of our mail and packages are handled by a post office.

A birthday card for Grandpa goes into the mailbox.

Busy postal workers weigh boxes and sell stamps so people can send letters, cards, and packages.

The postal worker puts the mail into bags.

Here comes the mail truck to pick up all the mail bags. The driver takes the mail to the sorting building.

A machine sorts the mail by address. There goes Grandpa's card! Some mail has to be sorted by hand.

The bags of sorted mail are taken all over the country in big mail trucks.

Airmail is taken all over the world by airplane.

Grandpa's birthday card has arrived in his town.

The mail carrier collects a bag of letters early in the morning.

The mail is sometimes delivered by bicycle.

Grandpa's card arrives at his home.

Happy birthday, Grandpa!

THE RESTAURANT

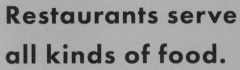
Restaurants serve
all kinds of food.

Diners wait for their tables to be ready.

A chef checks the fruit
and vegetables to make
sure they are fresh.

Dirty dishes
go into the
dishwasher.

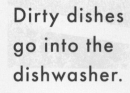

Inside, servers check the glasses, set the tables, and light the candles to get ready for the diners.

Servers hurry in with people's orders. Nobody wants cold soup!

The kitchen staff put on aprons, switch on the ovens, chop vegetables, wash fruit, clean fish, make sauces, beat eggs, and decorate desserts.

Everything must be just right. What a busy evening!

THE RAILROAD STATION

Railroad stations are busy places.

Signal controllers watch carefully to make sure each train goes along the right track.

Track inspectors wear brightly colored vests while they check the tracks for problems.

An engineer steers the train. A control panel in front can make the train go faster or slower.

On sleeper trains, a steward brings an early morning drink.

Conductors make sure the doors are closed tight. They blow their whistles to let the engineer know it is safe to pull out of the station.

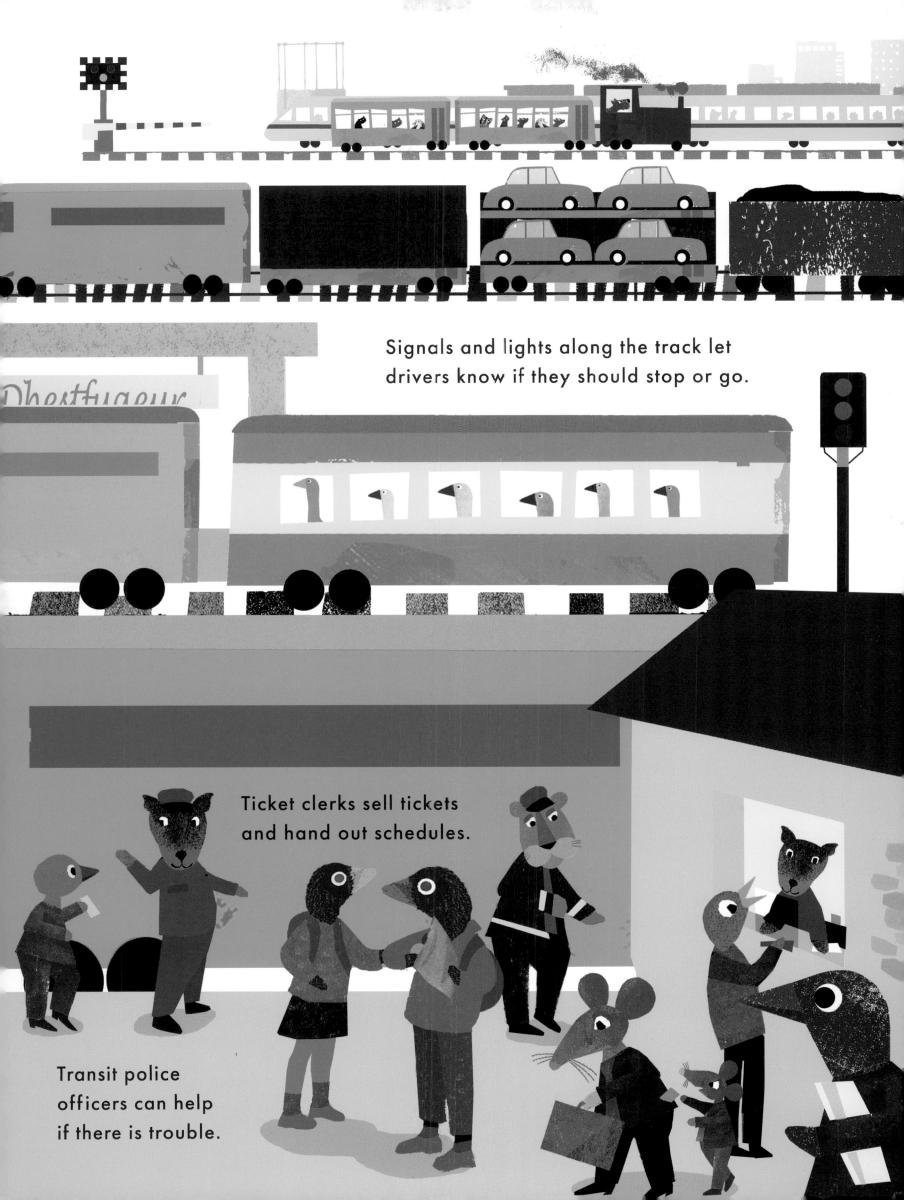

Signals and lights along the track let drivers know if they should stop or go.

Ticket clerks sell tickets and hand out schedules.

Transit police officers can help if there is trouble.

THE MUSEUM
This city is lucky enough to have a museum.

The museum curator is in charge of all the exhibits.

The staff check the air in the cabinets. If it's too damp, everything is ruined.

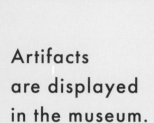

Artifacts are displayed in the museum.

A museum guide tells a group of visitors the story of how these dinosaur bones were found.

Technicians clean and restore everything very carefully.

An archaeologist finds fossils and sends them to the museum for investigation and display.

Artists have their work displayed in galleries for people to admire.

Museum guards make sure that no one touches the paintings.

Very old paintings need careful cleaning by the restoration staff.

Sometimes paintings and sculptures go to storage to make room for new ones.

An artist is having a successful show of his latest work.

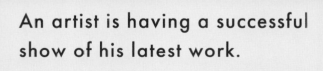